# The Chumash Indians

by Bill Lund

**Content Consultant:**
Jan Timbrook, Senior Associate Curator of Anthropology
Santa Barbara Museum of Natural History

## Bridgestone Books
an imprint of Capstone Press

Bridgestone Books are published by Capstone Press
818 North Willow Street, Mankato, Minnesota 56001
http://www.capstone-press.com

*Library of Congress Cataloging-in-Publication Data*
Lund, Bill, 1954-.
      The Chumash Indians/by Bill Lund
      p. cm. -- (Native peoples)
      Includes bibliographical references and index.
      Summary:  Discusses the Chumash Indians as a modern group with a unique history and
its own special practices and customs.
      ISBN 1-56065-562-3
      1.  Chumash Indians--History--Juvenile literature.  2.  Chumash Indians--Social life and
customs--Juvenile literature.
      [1. Chumash Indians.  2. Indians of North America--California]  I. Title.
      II. Series:  Lund, Bill, 1954-   Native peoples.

E99.C815L85  1998
979.4'004975--dc21
                                                          97-6395
                                                          CIP
                                                          AC

Photo credits
Betty Crowell, cover
Kent Christenson, 10
Santa Barbara Museum of Natural History, 8, 16, 20
Santa Ynez Indian Reservation, 6, 12
Bob Volpe, 18
Len Wood/Santa Barbara *News-Press*, 14

# Table of Contents

# Map

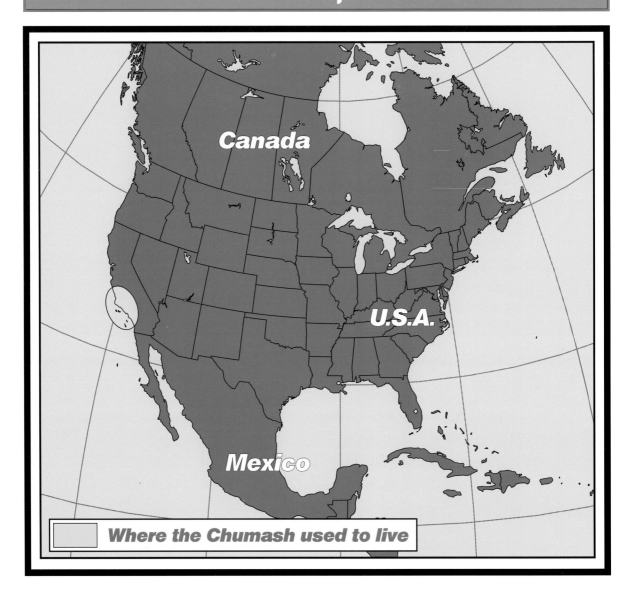

Canada

U.S.A.

Mexico

Where the Chumash used to live

# Fast Facts

Today, the Chumash Indians live like most other North Americans. In the past, they practiced a different way of life. Their food, homes, and clothing helped make them special. These facts tell how the Chumash once lived.

**Food**: The Chumash ate wild plants and seeds. They also ate fish, seafood, and animals.

**Home**: A Chumash house was round. It was called an 'ap. The Chumash made their houses from poles. They covered the poles with bulrush and cattail plants.

**Clothing**: Chumash men usually wore only a small carrying net and a belt. Chumash women wore skirts made from animal skins. Sometimes they made skirts from parts of plants.

**Language**: The Chumash had their own language.

**Past Location**: The Chumash have always lived in the same area. That area is now part of southern California.

**Current Location**: Many Chumash still live in southern California near Santa Barbara.

**Special Events**: The Chumash used to hold a harvest festival in early fall. They held a special ceremony in honor of the sun in winter. Songs and dances were part of many of their special events.

# The Chumash People

The Chumash have lived in southern California for more than 3,000 years. Many still live near the Santa Barbara area. In the past, there were between 15,000 and 20,000 Chumash. Today, there are about 3,000 Chumash.

Some Chumash live on the Santa Ynez reservation. A reservation is land set aside for Native Americans. Some people stay on the reservation their whole lives. Many others live and work outside of the reservation.

The Chumash people are working to save their history. They want people to remember and to learn from the past.

Some Chumash go to schools to teach students about Chumash history. They do traditional dances and tell stories. A tradition is a practice continued over many years.

**The Chumash are working to save their history.**

# Homes, Food, and Clothing

In the past, a Chumash house was called an 'ap. An 'ap was round with a round roof. The Chumash bent wooden poles together to make the houses. Then they covered the poles with bulrush and cattail plants.

The Chumash ate many plants. They ate fruit and berries. They also ate seeds and roots. Acorns were their most important food. Women mashed acorns into flour. They used the flour to make a type of soup. The Chumash also ate many kinds of fish and seafood. Chumash men hunted deer and other animals.

The weather in California is warm. The Chumash did not need to wear clothing for warmth. Men often wore nothing at all. Sometimes they wore a small net on a belt. They used the net to carry things. Women wore skirts made from animal skins or parts of plants.

In the past, a Chumash house was called an 'ap.

# The Chumash Family

Family is very important to the Chumash. In the past, they lived in large family groups. Fathers, mothers, and their children lived together. The husbands of married daughters lived with the family, too. Grandparents, aunts, uncles, and cousins could also live with the family.

Family members helped children become adults. Boys and girls learned by watching their parents. The children practiced making toy bows and arrows, baskets, and tools. Grandparents told stories that helped the children learn.

Today, parents, children, and grandparents often live together. Chumash women often make decisions for the families. Usually both parents work.

Family is very important to the Chumash.

# The Chumash Religion

The Chumash have their own religion. A religion is a set of beliefs people follow. Many spirits had power in the Chumash religion. The Chumash asked these spirits to help them. The most important spirit for the Chumash was the Sun. Other spirits were animals. The Chumash also prayed to thank the Earth for food.

Many Chumash villages had shamans. A shaman is a religious leader. The shaman was able to talk with the spirits. Spirits helped the shaman do things. Sometimes spirits helped shamans make sick people healthy.

Today, many Chumash are members of the Catholic church. The Catholic church is part of the Christian religion. Christianity is a religion based on the teachings of Christ. Some Chumash still follow the Chumash religion.

Some Chumash still follow the Chumash religion.

13

# Chumash Villages

In the past, the Chumash lived in villages. Large villages might have had more than 1,000 people. Each village had its own chief. The chief could be a man or a woman. Usually, the chief's father had been a chief, too. The chief made decisions for the village. The chief also kept extra supplies of food. He or she fed people when food was short.

The Chumash traded food and tools between villages. They also traded with other Native Americans in the area. They traded baskets, wooden and stone bowls, and canoes. The canoes were called tomols. Some Chumash made shell beads. The beads were their form of money.

Today, many Chumash live on the Santa Ynez reservation. The Chumash Business Council is the reservation government. All reservation members can vote on decisions made by the council.

The Chumash Business Council has a president.

# Chumash History

In the 1700s, Spanish people came to live in California. They changed the Chumash way of life. They wanted the Chumash to become Spanish citizens. They thought this would make the Chumash better people.

The Spanish wanted the Chumash to follow the Catholic religion. They set up religious villages called missions.

The Spanish brought many Chumash to live and work in the missions. Many Chumash became sick and died in the missions. Later, some Chumash worked for American settlers.

In 1901, the U.S. government set aside land for the Chumash. This land became known as the Santa Ynez reservation. Today, the Chumash are trying to bring back their past way of life. They are learning about their history and their traditions.

The Spanish set up villages called missions.

# Chumash Rock Paintings

The Chumash are famous for their paintings on cave walls. Many of the cave paintings had religious meaning.

The Chumash painted many things in nature. They made paintings of animals, fish, and birds. They also painted stars, lines, and many shapes. Some of the paintings are of spirits.

The Chumash made the paints from charcoal and colored rocks. Charcoal is made from burned wood. It is black.

The Chumash also used soft rocks that were red or white. They pounded these soft rocks into powders. Then they added water, plant sap, or animal fat. This made the rocks into paints.

The Chumash used plant leaves or animal tails as paint brushes. They also painted with their fingers.

The Chumash made paintings of things in nature.

# Chumash Legends

The Chumash told many stories to explain things in nature. These stories are called legends. Some Chumash stories taught the difference between right and wrong.

The Chumash believed that animals were once called the First People. Eagle was the Chief. Pelican was a fisher. Coyote was always getting into trouble.

One story tells about Coyote's marriage to Frogwoman. Frogwoman had control over water. One day Coyote caught many water birds. Instead of sharing with his family, he ate them all himself. This made Frogwoman angry. She dried up all of the rivers and lakes.

Coyote was very thirsty. He couldn't find any water. Finally, Frogwoman took pity on him. She brought the water back. This story teaches the Chumash not to be selfish.

**Storytellers still use legends to teach lessons.**

# Hands On: Ball Race

The Chumash enjoyed racing games. They played one game using balls. You can play this game, too.

## What You Need

two soccer balls
two teams

## What You Do

1. Choose a path for the race. You will need a starting point and an ending point.
2. Both teams start the race at the same time.
3. Team members move their ball toward the ending point. They use their feet to pass the ball to other members of their team.
4. The first team to kick the ball across the ending point wins.

## Words to Know

**'ap** (AHP)—a Chumash house made from poles covered with bulrush and cattail plants

**legend** (LEJ-uhnd)—a story told to explain things in nature or to teach a lesson

**mission** (MISH-uhn)—a religious village

**reservation** (rez-ur-VAY-shuhn)—land set aside for use by Native Americans

**shaman** (SHAH-muhn)—a religious leader

## Read More

**Duvall, Jill D**. *The Chumash*. Chicago: Children's Press, 1994.

**Schwabacher, Martin**. *The Chumash Indians*. New York: Chelsea House Publishers, 1995.

## Useful Addresses

**Chicken Ranch Chumash**
P.O. Box 1699
Jamestown, CA 95327

**Santa Ynez Chumash**
P.O. Box 517
Santa Ynez, CA 95327

## Internet Sites

**Chumash Frequently Asked Questions**
http://www.rain.org/~anthro/faq.htm

**Chumash Indians**
http://www.sbceo.k12.ca.us/~eagles/chumash.htm

## Index